LET'S MAKE WAV

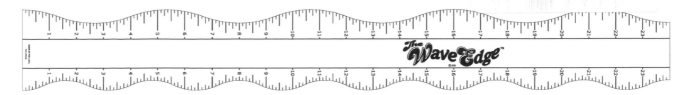

by

Lily Marie Amaru

Mission Statement
To encourage people to work
with their creative and intuitive nature.

Third Printing
September 2006

Inspirations by Lily Marie Publications

LET'S MAKE WAVES

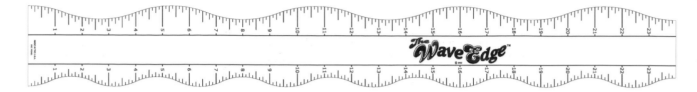

by Lily Marie Amaru

Illustrations & Design by Lily Marie Amaru

Photography by Burgess Photography, Gary Burgess

Contributors: Frances Farrand, Jancy Muensterman and June Owens

Editors: Claudia Bradley, Gai Loper, Linda Walden and Tamara Springfield

Library of Congress Cataloging in Publication Data
Amaru, Lily Marie
  Let's Make Waves/by Lily Marie
  ISBN 0-9744315-0-8
  1. Quilting. 2. Quilting--Art.
  3. Quilting--Patterns.
  1. Title.
Publisher:
    Inspirations by Lily Marie
    lilymarie@express56.com
    www.thewaveedgeruler.com
Printed in the U.S.A.

Table of Contents

Chapter 4
Assembly of Blocks..37

Chapter 5
Cover Quilt Instructions...41

Chapter 6
Borders, Edges and Binding..................................47

LET'S MAKE WAVES

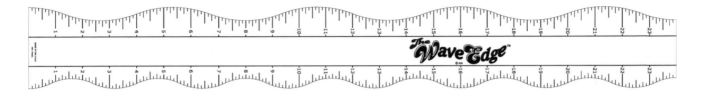

Dedicated to
Randy Schafer

Randy's faith and support in the beginning helped to bring The Wave Edge™ ruler from infancy to maturity.

Had it not been for Randy, the name of this ruler might have been "Innies and Outies." When I described the ruler to him in this way, he said, "OH! You mean like a wave?"

In Appreciation

I'd like to start my thanks with the lady who nudged the idea that had come to me about a ruler: Linda Mac Dougall. Thank you, Linda.

The support I have received from family and friends kept me moving forward towards a ruler patent, manufacturing, pattern and now this book. Thank you one and all.

Kathy Zerbey who was interested in the first wave quilt I made.

My son Kurt Schmitt who cut my first prototype ruler and did the logo.

Jane Garrison who gave me the name of Randy Schafer.

Randy's crew Dave Ray and E. J. Norgard, and Rulersmith employees, who worked with me from prototype to the finished ruler.

Carolyn Reese from the Road to California, who helped with the type of measurement markings and let me introduce The Wave Edge™ ruler at the 2003 Road to California Quilt Show.

My friends Claudia Bradley, Roy Shea, and Linda Walden who helped in proofing my instructions for the ruler. Linda also encouraged me to get the web site started and then did the work of getting it put together and up and running: www.thewaveedgeruler.com.

Tammie Bowser for doing the leg work to lead me to the printer of this book.

Maggie McDermott for giving me my title "The Wave Diva". Bobbie Moon who shared her knowledge of packaging.

Dick Tristao who helped with the continued instructions on Abobe Page Maker and Corel Draw.

Gary Burgess for the many trips to the ocean for the front and back cover of this book. And for all the ladder work for the pictures on the inside of the book.

To Gai, Claudia, Linda and Tamara for the editing of this book. Somedays it wasn't easy.

To all who encouraged me with words and thoughts, customers who have and have not bought the ruler, Beverly Shea, Sharon Graff, Nancy Auch, Mickey Stone, Ellie Eck, Lynne Launius. And all my friends from Designing Ladies of Burbank.

Jancy, Frances, Marty and June for their lovely quilts and projects featured in the color section of this book.

Keepsake Quilting who named this book from the ad in their catalog.

My gift to be able to listen to my creativity and intuition, and the courage to walk through the open doors.

The ruler is truly a gift.

Introduction

Curves have been around for a long time. For example, Drunkards Path, a <u>real</u> curve.

Quilters like Judy B. Dales whose book "Curves in Motion" inspired me to play with curves in the first place. Judy, I never did get it. What it inspired in me has been truly more fun than I could have imagined.

Many find working with curves a real challenge. Others are reluctant to try it. New words have been brought to the way we communicate about those challenges; (working outside your box or your envelope). Here is hoping that my ruler will do what we used to have to do free hand and will take some of the challenge out of curves.

Over the years many designers and instructors have taught curves. Some with exaggerated twists and turns such as Judy's work which is so amazing and leaves me with much awe in how they did it. The motion of this kind of curve is wonderfully pleasing to the eye. Some free form curves have been established within a block by many people.

Today the quilter who wants flow and movement in their quilts now have a tool to accomplish this. They can do this with squares or strips simply by cutting, clipping, pinning, sewing, and pressing.

The Wave Edge™ ruler came from the need to hold the fabric in place while being cut with a rotary cutter and a desire to have consistancy in my work.

Quilters and designers are finding many uses for the ruler. Uses I would never have expected.

I expectation this will be one of many books that will be published using The Wave Edge™ ruler.

"It is a Grand and Glorious New Day
in which to Excel "

Thank you friend; it is.

"Enrich your quilting creativity"

Linda Walden

Chapter 1

Getting Started

"Trust ...
the process"

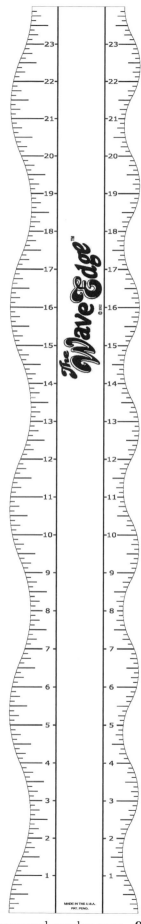

Anatomy of the ruler

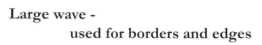

Ruler length 24"

Large wave -
used for borders and edges

Small wave - used to construct blocks

24" end - used on the fold of fabric to give
a full valley

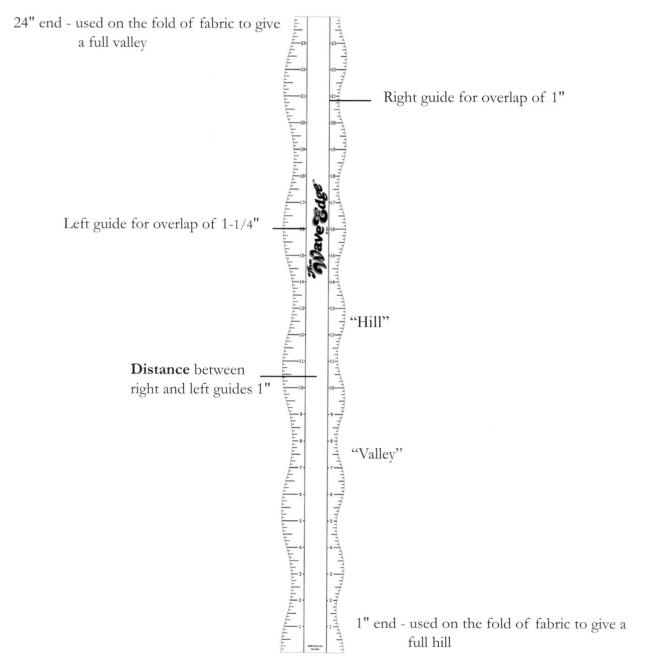

Right guide for overlap of 1"

Left guide for overlap of 1-1/4"

"Hill"

Distance between
right and left guides 1"

"Valley"

1" end - used on the fold of fabric to give a
full hill

FEATURES	BENEFITS
24 inches long	To cut entire width of folded fabric
One end valley	To create full valley at fold of fabric
One end hill	To create full hill at fold of fabric
Depth of hill and valley consistant	To keep momentum of design going to outside edge of quilt or wall hanging
Ruler markings	To allow for specific designs
Longer waves	To create symmetrical edges or quilting designs

The Wave Edge™ ruler can be used for

Piecing
Borders
Symmetrical curved edges - quilts and garments
Wearables
Markings for quilting and vines
Applique
Facings on garments, quilts, and linens
Use your imagination!

SUGGESTED SUPPLIES

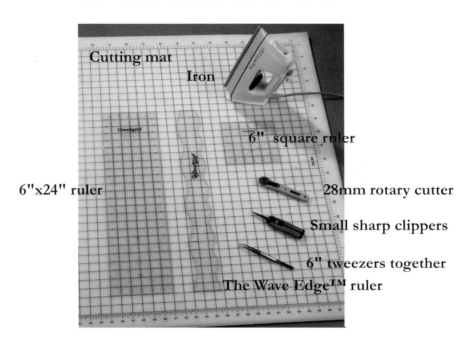

Cutting mat

Iron

6" square ruler

6"x24" ruler

28mm rotary cutter

Small sharp clippers

6" tweezers together

The Wave Edge™ ruler

SUPPLIES NOT SHOWN

Invisi-Grip..Keep ruler from sliding
Large rotary cutter...Cutting strips
1/4" Presser foot..Sewing
Spray starch or sizing..Pressing seams
Stiletto..In place of tweezers
Fine quilting pins...Pinning the hills to the valleys

Chapter 2

Ruler Basics/Using the Ruler

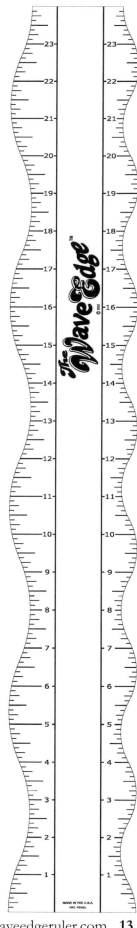

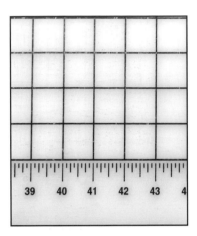

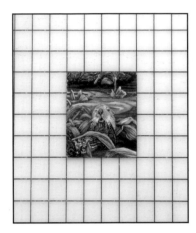

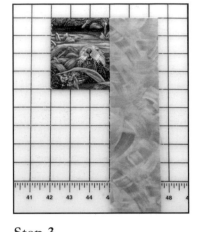

Step 1

Use an accurate 1" square mat.

Step 2

Start with a minimum 3" square: fussy cut or not.

. Place block right side up with right edge on a vertical 1" grid line.

Step 3

Place first strip right side up overlapping square by 1". This overlap is the one constant throughout the cutting of the quilt, blocks, strips, and putting the blocks together.

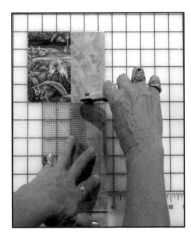

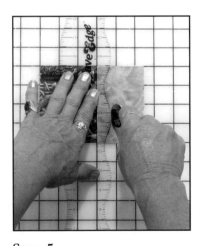

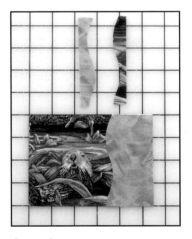

Step 4

Trim strip to the same length as block

Step 5

Place The Wave Edge™ ruler with right guide line on top strip of fabric., Tip 28mm rotary cutter slighty to the right and cut along The WaveEdge™ ruler. **Hint: if your mat is old and has deep groves from cutting, you may not have a clean cut.**

Step 6

The small pieces are the cuts Throw away or donate to local teachers for school projects.

Step 7

Place right sides together with hills on hills and valleys on valleys. Just for clipping.

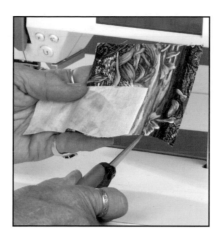

Step 8

Clip the valleys 1/8" deep, making about four or five clips in each valley. **Hint: Mark clippers with a dot of finger nail polish 1/8" in from the tips for accuracy.**

Step 9

Place pieces back together right sides up to recreate the square, snuggling the hills to the valleys.

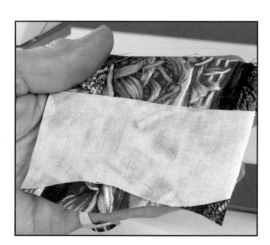

Step 10

Flip small strip so right sides are together, the hills on top of the valleys.

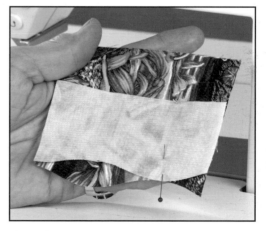

Step 11

Pin the hills to the valleys. **Hint: Pinning the entire length of the wave is optional.**

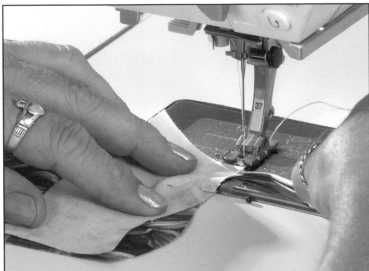

Step 12

Using the tweezers bring the upper edge of the top fabric to the upper edge of the bottom fabric. **Hint: Handling the pieces, I use the ring finger and pinky of my left hand to slightly move the bottom fabric to line it up with My index and middle fingers are supporting the top fabric.**

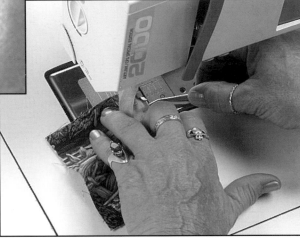

Step 13

Raise the presser foot and slide the pieces under the foot. Lower presser foot. Lower the needle into the fabric and take a couple securing stitches.

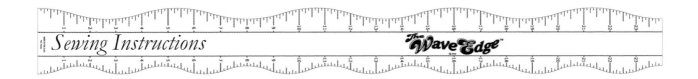

Step 14

After taking the securing stitches, raisepresser foot to let the fabric relax. Bring the fabrics together using thetweezers. **Hint: You are always bringing valleys to hills. If the valley is on the bottom, use the tweezers to bring the bottom fabric to the hill is on the top. If the valley is on the top, bring the top fabric with the tweezers to the hill on the bottom.**

Step 15

Lower presser foot.
Pull first pin and continue to sew.

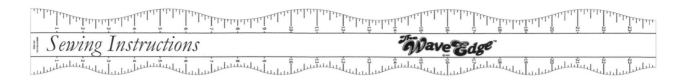

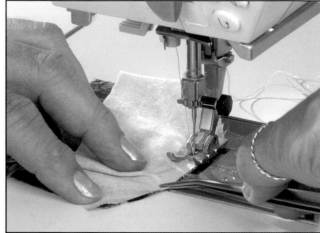

Step 16

Finish seam, bringing the valley edges to

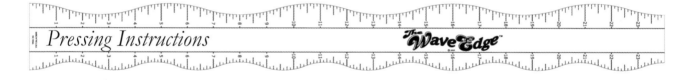
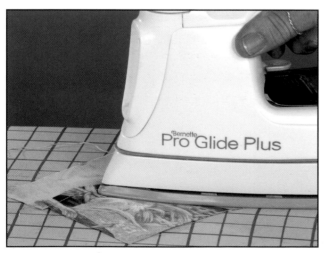

Step 17
With seam side up, press seam towards the piece you sewed on. Using steam is ok.

Step 18
Turn piece over and press, moving the iron from center of block to strip that was sewn on last.

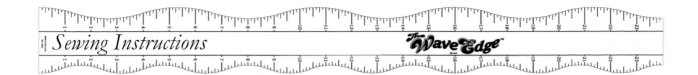
Look at your block. If the added strip does not perfectly match the edges of the center square, do not worry. Fabric has a tendency to shift a bit whenever you sew. You never need to clean up this edge. As you add new strips to the block, the little tails or imperfections of sewing are cut away. **HINT: You can somewhat alleviate these imperfections by raising and lowering your presser foot more often, relaxing the fabric as you sew.**

Place block face up on cutting mat and line up the next edge of the center square with a vertical grid line. Following instructions numbered 2-18, add three more strips to the center block.

You now have a center square with one complete row of strips added. This block will probably not be square. It's OK!!!!! It is supposed to be like this. And your block may have little ripples along the outside edge. This is OK too!!! This is a very forgiving technique.

To add more rows around the block, start by laying the block face up on the cutting mat with the right edge along a 1" vertical grid line. Look at the block. If it does not appear straight to you, shift the block slightly so it straightens out.

After shifting the block, the right edge will probably no longer totally lie along the vertical grid line. Just make sure some point of the block always stays along the veritical line. Again, follow instructions 2-18. Interestingly, as you continue to sew more strips around the block, the block lays flatter.

IMPORTANT: The only time you square up any block using a ruler is after you have sewn all the blocks required by your pattern. This is covered in Chapter 4.

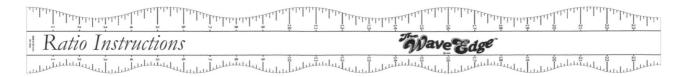
You can use The Wave Edge™ ruler in any pattern that calls for strip piecing. Cut the strips 3/4" wider than the size called for in the pattern. For example, if the pattern calls for a 1-1/2" strip you will cut your strips 2-1/4" wide (unfinished 1-1/2" plus 3/4").

Because of the randomness of cutting the wave and your own unique 1/4" seam, the finished wave blocks will vary from the size noted in the pattern. You may want to make a few test blocks.

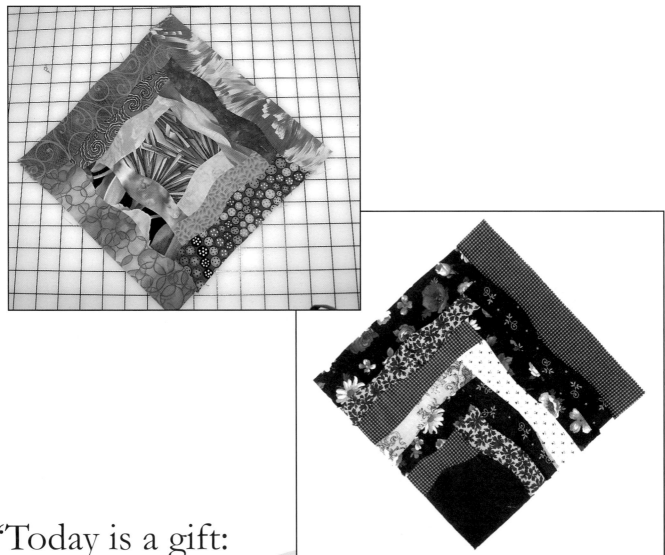

"Today is a gift:
Honor it by fully living in it."

The most common OOPS in using The Wave Edge™ ruler is putting the two pieces of fabric right sides together, instead of both right sides up. Here is how to fix it: discard the top strip that was face down. Keep the orginal block.

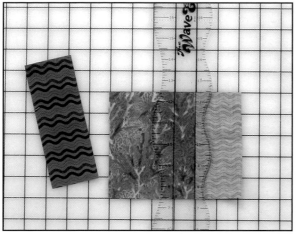

Step 1
The strip off to the left shows the fabric right side up. The strip under the ruler, ready to be cut, is wrong side up.

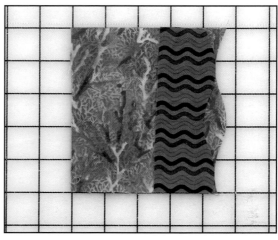

Step 2
OOPS!!!!!!!!!! You realize that you cut wrong and have to throw away the strip.

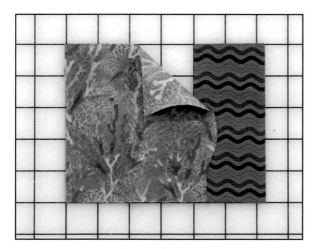

Step 3
Without moving the block, fold back the right edge to place a new strip on the vertical grid line used when you made the OOPS!!!!!!!!!! Replace the cut block on top of strip.

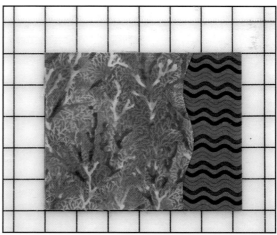

Step 4
Line up the ruler with the wave in the block. Cut bottom strip and sew.

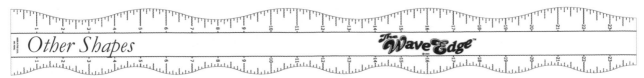

The Wave Edge™ ruler can be used in creating new fabric for cutting squares, triangles, circles, applique pieces, and spirals. Use your imagination.

Step 1

Place a full fabric width folded only once wrong sides together on a 1" grid line.

Step 2

Place a second strip folded only once wrong sides together on top of the bottom fabric aligning folded edges. Follow step 3 on page 14

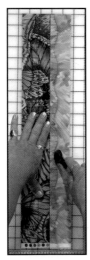

Step 3

Lay either end of the ruler on the fold. Cut. NOTE: For staggered waves, use opposite end of the ruler on the folded end of alternate cuts

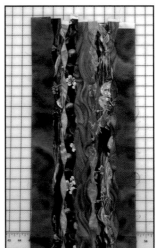

Step 4

Continue adding strips to make a strata to any desired width. Use to cut new shapes.

Have Fun!!!!!!!!!!

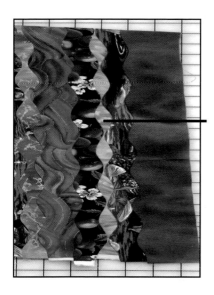

Peek-a-boo strip - can be used in blocks or strata.

When making the vest on page 32. I happened to cut one of the strips at 2". As I was going to make my overlap and cut, I noticed that if I placed the ruler with the center of the valley to the center of the hill I could get this Peek-a-Boo effect. Now you can benefit by my boo boo!!!

Step 1
The peek-a-boo strip is going to be 2" wide. First strip can be any width from 2-1/2" to 6". Follow steps 3 and 5 on page 14 for cutting.

Step 2
The left edge of the next strip will lay next to the hills of the first strip.

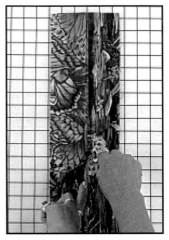

Step 3

Place edge of ruler with the bottom of valley at the top of the sewn hill. Cut.

Step 4

Cut made.

Step 5
Prep to sew.
IMPORTANT: This is the only time the newly added piece will be on the bottom as you sew. You need to see the smallest piece to ensure the seams at the top of the hills do not overlap.

Step 6
Press seam away from the Peek-a-Boo fabric. Flip strips and press. See the the Peek-a-Boo effect.

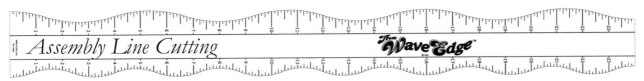

Step 1
Place blocks on mat one above another

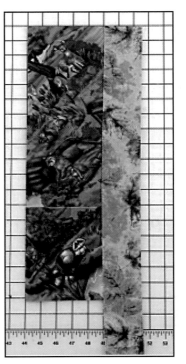

Step 2
Place strip on all blocks overlapping 1". Cut strip the same length as blocks.

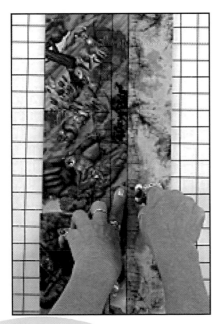

Step 3
Place ruler using step 5 on page 14.

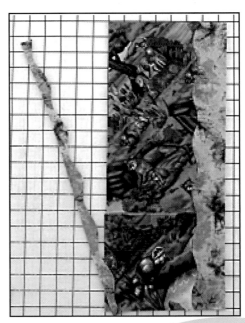

Step 4
Remove long strip and discard.

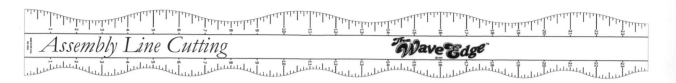
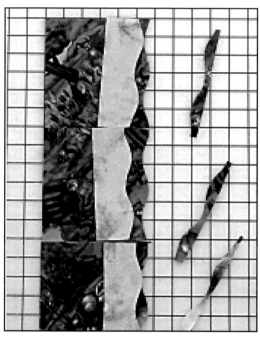

Step 5
Using small ruler, cut long strip in between blocks.

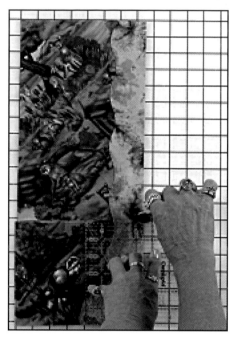

Step 6
Flip strips to right side of blocks and discard cut away block strips. Prep to sew.

"Whether you think you can, or think you can't... you're right"

Henry Ford

Chapter 3

Quilts, Wearables & Projects

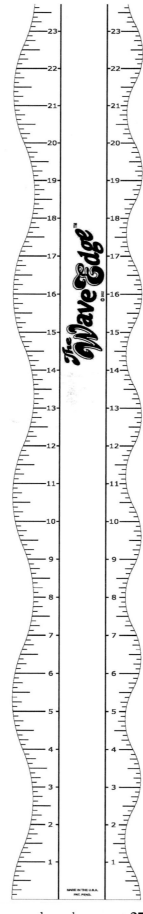

Designer Lily Marie "The Wave Diva"

Designer Lily Marie "The Wave Diva"

"In the beginning ....
the Spirit moved over the waters."

Designer Marty Rehm

Designer Lily Marie "The Wave Diva"

Lotus Wave pattern available

Back art

All Designs on this page by Designer Lily Marie "The Wave Diva"

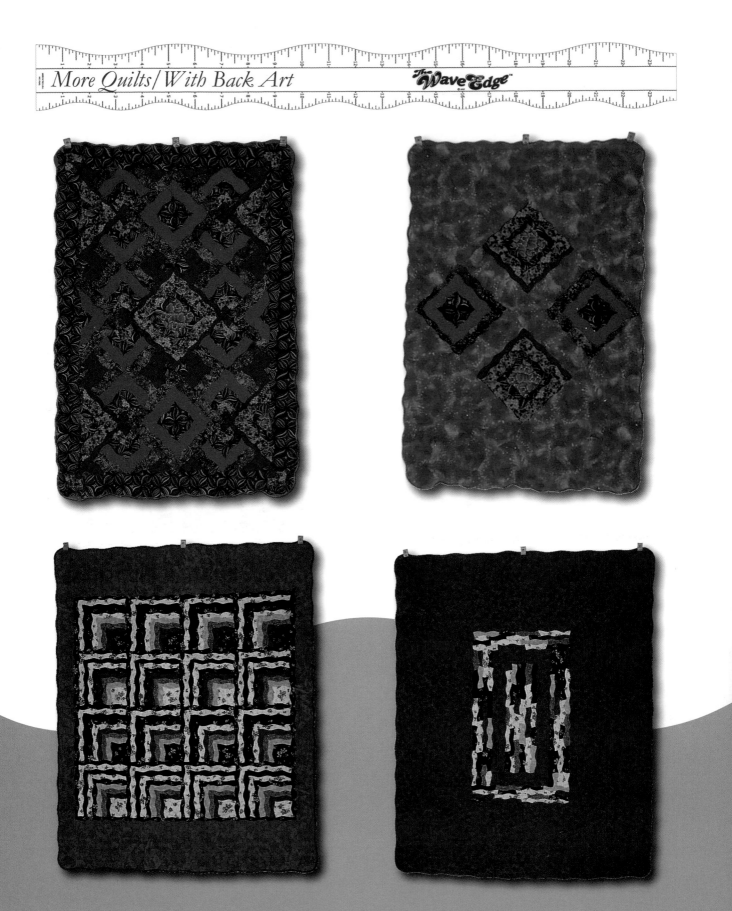

All Designs on this page by Designer Lily Marie "The Wave Diva"

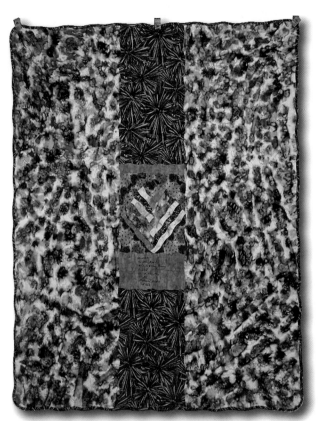

Designer Lily Marie "The Wave Diva"   Designer Lily Marie "The Wave Diva"

Designer Jancy Muensterman

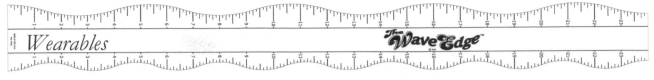

Designer Lily Marie Amaru

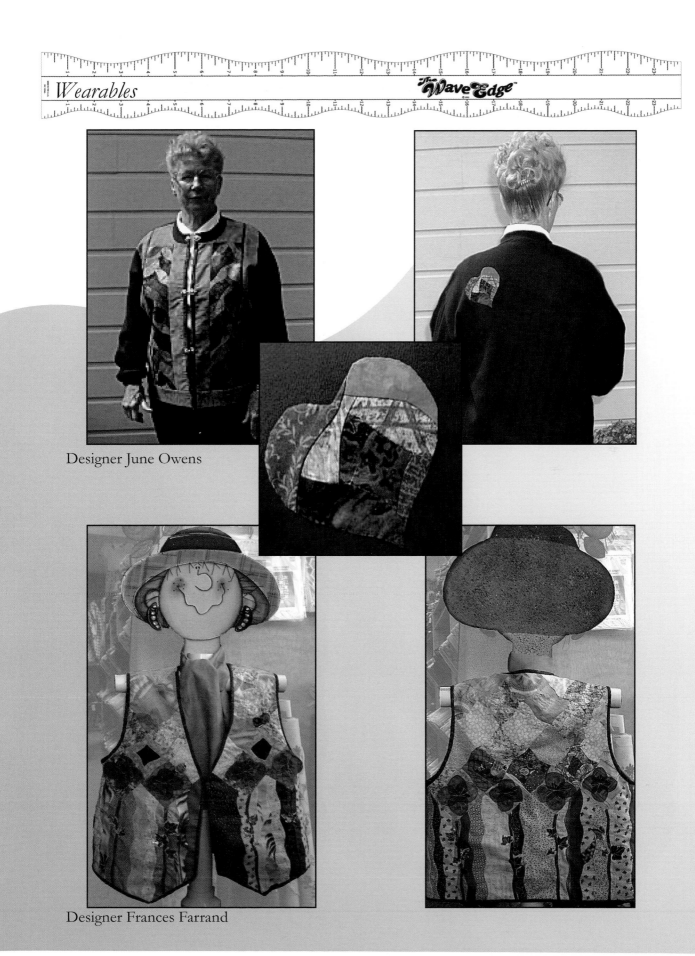

Designer June Owens

Designer Frances Farrand

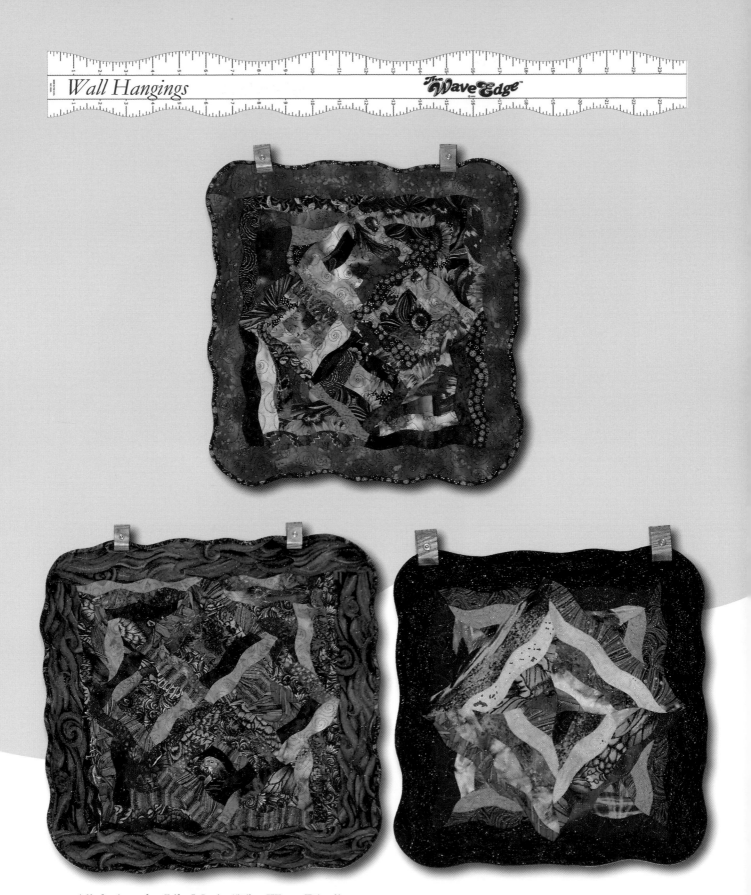

All designs by Lily Marie "The Wave Diva"

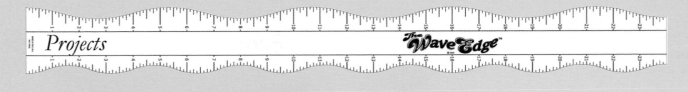

Place mat and napkin by Lily Marie "The Wave Diva"

Pillow case by Lily Marie "The Wave Diva"

Claudia's Bag by Lily Marie "The Wave Diva"

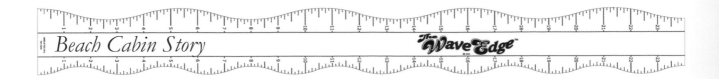

Thank you Deanna Bond.

When I do my demos of the ruler at shows I like to have fun and tell the consumer that we are going to put the hill to the valleys to make waves. Most of the time the consumer is so involved with my demo that they don't hear what I have said. One day at the San Diego Quilt show Deanna was watching me do a demo using my comments of the hills and valleys becoming waves. She said, "so you can have a Beach Cabin".

I asked her for her name and we quickly bonded with our life stories. What a wonderful world we live in that we can make deep relationships in moments by the fun things in life that we say.

My quilts that have log cabins will now be called Beach Cabins. How appropriate as I live in California I love the beach and the hills and valleys.

Chapter 4

Assembly of Blocks

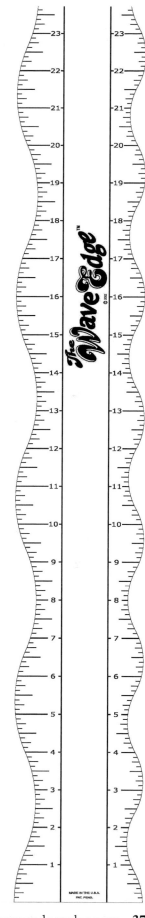

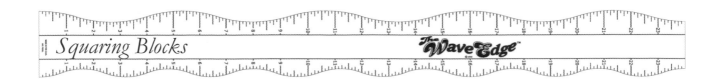

Step 1
Find the smallest block in the group.

Step 2
The measurements of the smallest block
 will dictate the size of the rest of your blocks.

Step 3
Square up as you normally would.

"Try a Dose of ...
Laughter"

Step 1

Place all blocks on flannel board according to pattern. Start with two blocks from the first row and follow the rest of the steps in the assembly section.

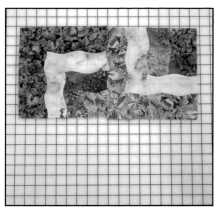

Step 2

Place first block on a 1" grid line, place 2nd block on top of first block over lapping 1". Right sides up. Cut with ruler; sew and press.

Step 3

Place the two sewn blocks on the mat bottom edge on a 1" grid line. Bring in next two blocks as you did the first two, overlap the top of these two blocks on the top blocks 1". Place ruler on top of blocks lining up the waves of ruler with the waves of the blocks already sewn. Remove the top blocks leaving the ruler in place .

Step 4

Ruler is in place. Cut, clip, sew and press

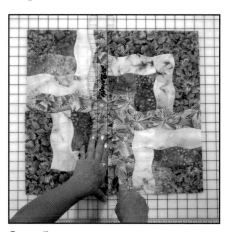

Step 5

Take both sets of blocks and over lap 1". Place ruler so that either a full hill or valley is where the seam lines match. This will make it easier to match the seams for sewing. The rest of your quilt will be put together in this manner.

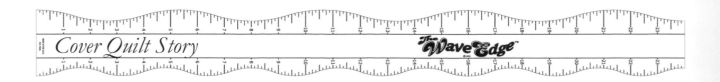

When our lives start we never know where the path may lead us.

We meet many people along this path. Some stay as they should and others are just there for a short time.

I have been blessed with a friend Beverly, who came into my life when I was just six years old. Our paths took us to different places for about twenty years.

When it was about time for Beverly's fiftieth birthday, I decided it was time we started to communicate again. I called her and we have been in close contact, just like the old days. She has come to California and I have been to her new home in Indiana. She calls her place McShea's Fairie Ridge.

My first year 2003 of doing Festival in Chicago I thought it would be fun to have Beverly come and work with me. It would give us time to catch up and she could see me in action. We had a great time.

I asked her if I were to make her something, what would she like? I gave her a few choices; wall hanging, place mats or a lap quilt. She said place mats, so she could put them on her patio table. I decided that I didn't want my work on a table outside. So it was settled, a wall hanging or lap quilt was the project.

Once I started working on my book, I knew I needed to have a quilt pattern in it. I decided to make two different Beach Cabin blocks. With that decision made, the fairy fabric showed up in one of the stores where I teach. Guess who it was for? That's right, Beverly is getting her lap quilt.

As we quilters do, I bought a couple of yards of each color. I also mixed some of my stash (we all have some of that around) with the new collection.

I was invited to appear on Kaye Wood's quilting show, "Kaye's Quilting Friends". With a couple of blocks made and the pieces to work on, Beverly's fairy quilt was started on the show.

When the photographer, Gary, and I went to the beach to take my portrait, I picked up Beverly's quilt just in case the right moment came to take a good picture. The opportunity came and we took advantage of it.

Gary did a great job at catching the waves lapping at the corner of the quilt. It did get caught in the waves and pulled into the ocean, but was quickly rescued!. Beverly says that makes it all the more special.

When I told Beverly that her quilt was going to be on the cover of the book, she was and still is very excited.

Beverly and I have given the gift of friendship to each other.

Chapter 4

Cover Quilt Instructions

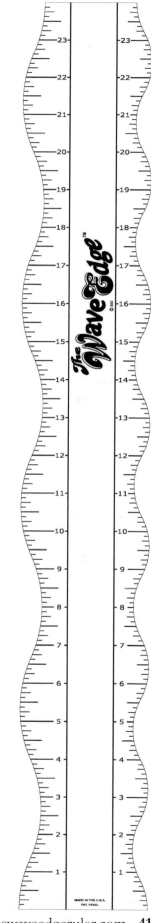

Block 1

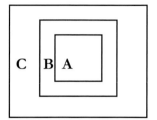

Color A: 1 1/2 yards
 Used in blocks, borders and
 back art.

Color B: 1 3/4 yards
 Used in blocks, border and
 back art.

Color C: 1 1/4 yards
 Used in blocks.

Color D: 1 1/2 yards
 Used in blocks, border and
 back art.

Color E: 2 yards
 Used in blocks, border,
 back art and binding.

Color F: 3 yards
 Used in back and border.

Block 2

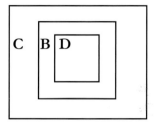

Block 3

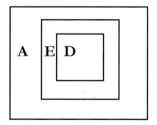

Block 4

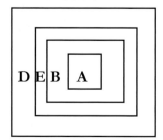

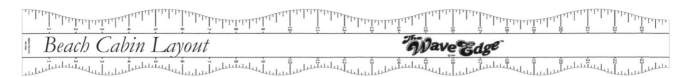

Block 1

    Pink Center Color A

        Cut 3 6" center blocks

        Fussy cut if you choose

    First round Color B

        Cut strips 3 1/2"

    Second round Color C

        Cut strips 3 1/2"

Block 2

    White Center Color D

        Cut 3 6" center blocks

        Fussy cut if you choose

    First round Color B

        Cut strips 3 1/2"

    Second round Color C

    Cut strips 3 1/2"

Block 3

    White Center Color D

        Cut 4 6" center blocks

        Fussy cut is you choose

    First round Color E

        Cut strips 3 1/2"

    Second round Color A

        Cut strips 3 1/2"

Block 4

    Pink Center Color A

        Cut 2 6" center blocks

        Fussy cut if you choose

    First round Color B

        Cut strips 2 1/2"

    Second round Color E

        Cut strips 3 1/2"

    Third round Color D

        Cut strips 2 1/2"

Block 1, 2 and 3

Make three copies of this block

Block 4

Make one copy of this block

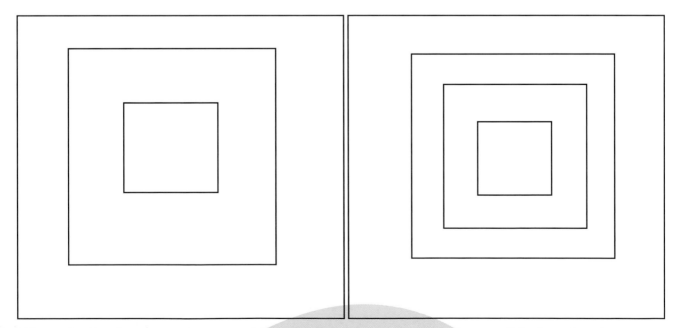

Permission is given to copy these blocks to use to paste your fabric selections on.

The quilt blocks for this quilt are arranged with the blocks on point. This arrangement will require you to cut some of your blocks into a triangle.

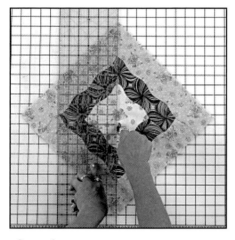

Blocks that will need to be cut into triangles are
Block 1 Cut two of these into triangles
Block 2 Cut one of these into a triangle
Block 4 Cut two of these into triangles

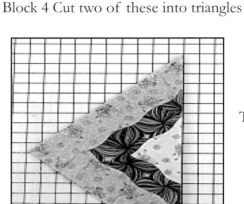

Triangle cut

Step 1
Lay block so that the points are on a grid line of the mat vertically. Using your straight edge ruler, cut into a triangle.

The rest of the top will be assembled as you would put the blocks together on pages 26 and 27.

You will do rows and then place them together so the rows are on point. See picture on page 30.

You can start in the top left hand corner if you choose, sewing two triangles together, next row will be triangle two full blocks and a triangle, third row is a triangle three full blocks and a triangle, fourth row is a triangle two blocks and a triangle, last row will be two triangles.

The following chapter will give you the information for the border and binding.

The back will also be covered in the next chapter.

"Live Life as an Opportunity"

Lily Marie Amaru

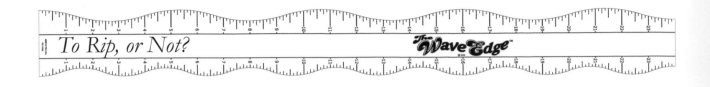

Perfect timing is when circumstances meet expectations

by Lily Marie *"The Wave Diva"*

Chapter 5

Borders, Edges and Bindings

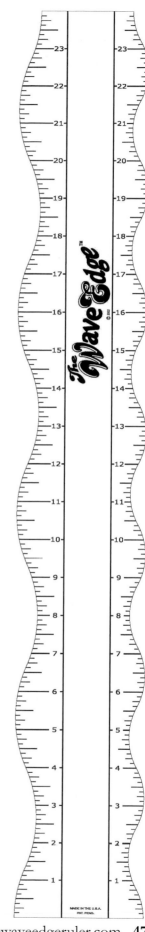

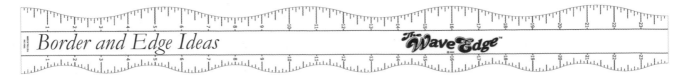

Cover quilt, border is done with spiral tubing see pages 49 to 51.

Lotus Wave pattern has a plain border, using long wave.

Edge using double cut wave page 53.

Border done with spiral tube.

Cover quilt border

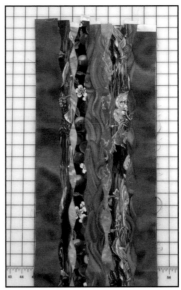

Step 1

Make a strada following instructions on page 22.

Step 2

Fold one end into a triangle. Using your 6x24" ruler, trim the edge.

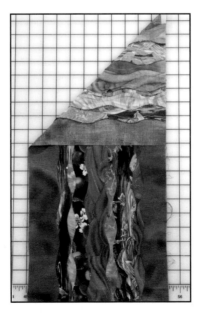

Picture 1   Right

Picture 2   Left

Step 3

To start the spiral, leave end folded in the triangle and place a pin in the lower corner on the outer edge. **Folding either right or left will give the spiral a different 45 degree angle.**

Spiral border instruction with the permission of Linda F. McGehee

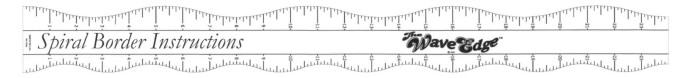

Step 4

Bring the fabric at the end of the fold on the left side of the strada to the right side of the strada to begin a tube. Sew with a long basting stitch.

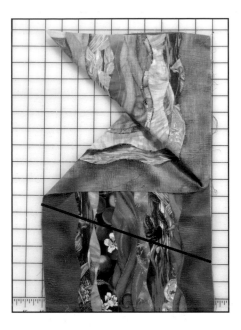

Step 5

Continue until you have sewn strada into a tube.

Step 6

Tube of strada.

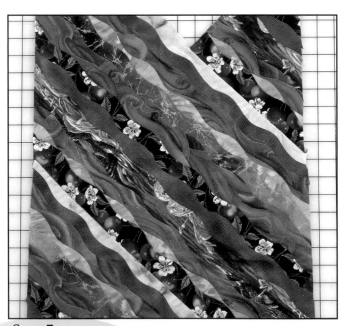

Step 7

Cut tube. Take basting seam out and make a wave seam.

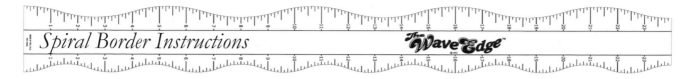
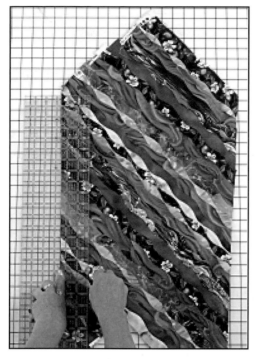

Step 8
Cut strips with straight edge ruler to desired widths.

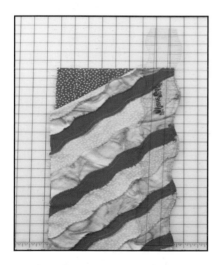

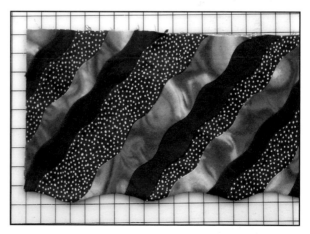

Facing for garments or ruffles, etc.
Using strada and a plain fabric
right sides together, use
The Wave Edge ™ ruler along
on straight edge. Cut then sew
1/4" seam and turn.

Refer to picture on page 35 in the color section
Pillow case. Also colorful vest on page 32.

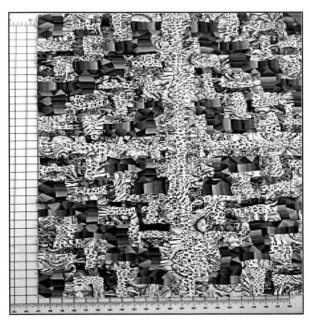

Step 1

Square up the quilt.

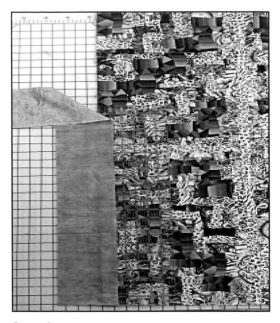

Step 2

To use the long wave, overlap
the quilt with border by an 1 1/4".

Step 3

For cutting accuracy, place The Wave Edge™
ruler long wave edge on border with guideline
on quilt edge. It helps to use a 24 x 6 ruler
straight edge on the guideline.
Follow directions on page 15 to finish.

Place the line closest to the longer wave
on the quilt edge and cut. Do sides first
then top and bottom.

**For a larger project use a 24 x 6 ruler
to keep the border, quilt and The Wave™
ruler straight. Clip and sew as you would a
block. Layer quilt and quilt.**

Border will be sewn just like you would
for a block see pages 15 to 19 Steps 7
to 18.

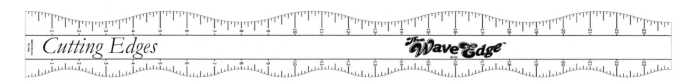
Cutting the edge can be done with either long wave or short wave

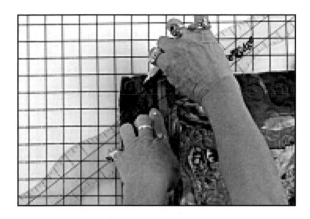

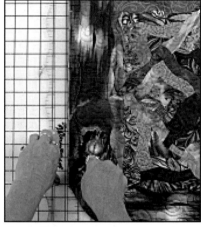

Step 1
Lay edge of long wave on the corner, using the long hill cut.

Step 2
Move ruler to sides, cut edge, fudging if necessary between corners.

Cutting Double Wave Edge

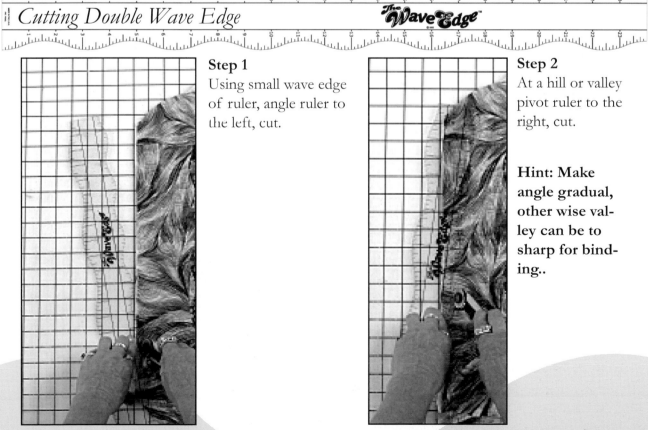

Step 1
Using small wave edge of ruler, angle ruler to the left, cut.

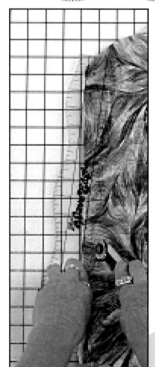

Step 2
At a hill or valley pivot ruler to the right, cut.

Hint: Make angle gradual, other wise valley can be to sharp for binding..

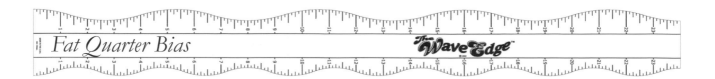
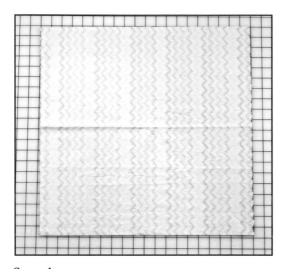

Step 1

Lay fat quarter on mat wrong side up.

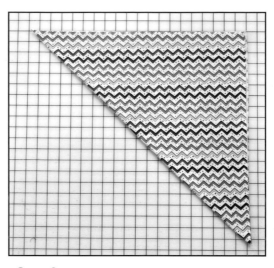

Step 2

Bring lower left hand corner to upper right hand corner making a triangle.

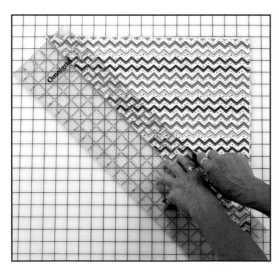

Step 3

Lay 6x24" ruler on fold at the 1 7/8" line, cut.

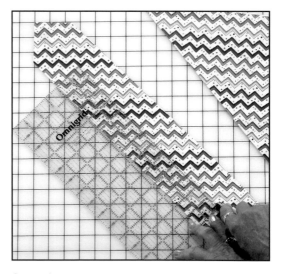

Step 4

Unfold first cut and lay 6x24" ruler on the 1 7/8" line, make next cut.

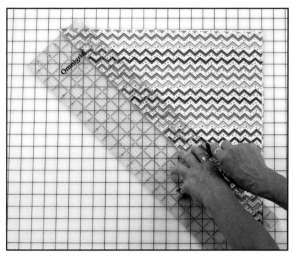

Step 5
Continue to cut bias from the rest of
the fat quarter.

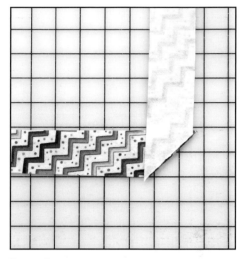

Step 6
Bias strips will come out ready to sew
into a long strip. This method will give
you less seams than the tube of the past.

"When you least expect it, life gives
you wonderful surprises"

Lily Marie Amaru

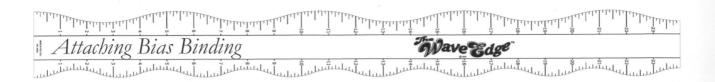

Step 1
Fold bias

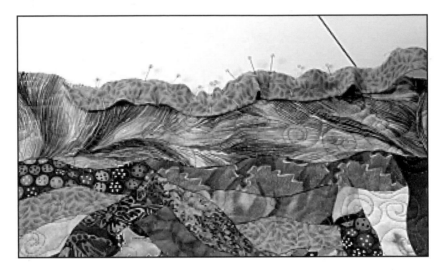

Step 2
Attach binding to edge of quilt. Do not stretch binding.

Step 3
Ease around corners

Steps 4 and 5
Sew with 1/4" seam.
Turn to back and hand sew.

"Breathe"

Project sheet

Project	Date of start/finish	Pattern	Yardage of fabric	Fabric samples	Fabric samples	Fabric samples
			Design	Designs	Borders	Back
			Borders		Sashing	Binding
		Picture of finished project	Back			
			Binding		Batting	
			Batting			
			Number of blocks			
			Style 1			
			Style 2			
			Style 3			
			Block size			
			Style 1			
		Notes	Style 2			
			Style 3			
			Finished size			

Permission given to copy this page for personal use only.

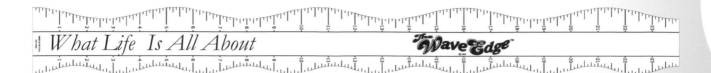

My life is a sacred journey, it is about change, growth, discovery, movement, transformation, continuously expanding my vision of what is possible, stretching my soul, learning to see clearly and deeply, listening to my intuition, taking courageous risks, and embracing challenges at every step along the way.

I am on my path exactly where I am meant to be right now...

Living my life in the present and planning for the future.

From here, I can only go forward, shaping my life into a magnificent story of triumph, healing, courage, beauty, wisdom, power, dignity and love.

9/27/01
Inspired by Caroline Joy Adams
Your Life is a Sacred Journey

Lily Marie's Adaptation

Lily Marie Amaru
"The Wave Diva"

I have been sewing since I was 10 years old. Garments have always been my focus until 2002 when I decided to make quilting my focus.

Much of what I have learned has been self taught. In the mid 70's I started to work for a sewing store. They needed a teacher and it seemed right since I had been sewing most of my life.

My first class that I taught was lingerie. I was so scared my voice even changed. Now it seems like second nature to give lectures and teach.

My teaching skills have covered everything from lingerie to mens wear. Teaching features of the sewing machine has been my speciality for most of my 27 years of teaching.

For 18 years I owned a sewing machine store on the Central Coast of California and spent another five years working for a major sewing machine company.

My pieced garments have been accepted by the Hoffman Challenge as part of their yearly traveling exhibitions. Over the years a number of my articles on garment sewing and techniques were published in Treadle Art, Martha Pullen's Sew Beautiful, and various Bernina Publications.

In 2002, I created The Wave Edge™ Ruler. This innovative method of cutting and piecing curves has been well accepted amongst the quilting world and made lots of waves along the way.

In May, 2003 I filmed a segment for Kaye Wood's "Kaye's Quilting Friends". In August, 2003, Quilting Professional featured The Wave Edge™ ruler and this "Wave Diva".

In December 2003, I was a guest on Simply Quilts HGTV, to be aired starting sometime in 2004.

Though I never stray far from my roots in garment sewing, I now travel and teach wave ruler methods extensively throughout the quilting community.

I have broken many of the quilting rules. I didn't know them. Sew isn't that ok? HA!

Again TRUST THE PROCESS.

Printed in the U.S.A at
Jostens Inc, Commercial Printing
Visalia, California
www.jostens.com/commercialprinting

Layout and Design by Lily Marie Amaru
lilymarie@express56.com

Finish Design and Digital Perparation by
Dick Tristao's TwoBitGrafix
Visalia, California
twobitgrafix@comcast.net

Order additional books and supplies:

Telephone orders: Call 909 389-4956   email orders: lilymarie@express56.com

ITEM	PRICE	QTY	SUBTOTAL
Rulers:			
The Wave Edge™ Ruler	$18.00		
16" Wave Edge™ Ruler	$17.50		
Simple Circles Ruler	$19.98		
Long Arm Machine	$34.00		
Patterns:			
The Wave Lotus	$ 8.00		
Scrappy Wave Pattern	$ 8.00		
Tri Angle Waves Pattern	$ 8.00		
Waves in the Rail Pattern	$ 8.00		
Circles of Colors Pattern	$ 8.00		
Waves of Placemats/ Napkins Pattern	$ 8.00		
Books:			
Let's Make Waves	$24.00		
Tools:			
Invisi Grip	$ 6.00		
Tweezers 6"	$ 3.50		
	Total Items Price		
	CA. residents add 8.25% CA Tax		
	Total		

Name _____

Address _____

City _____ State _____ ZIP _____

Phone _____

Email _____

Prices subject to change without notice.

Order additional books and supplies:

Telephone orders: Call 909 389-4956   email orders: lilymarie@express56.com

ITEM	PRICE	QTY	SUBTOTAL
Rulers:			
The Wave Edge™ Ruler	$18.00		
16" Wave Edge™ Ruler	$17.50		
Simple Circles Ruler	$19.98		
Long Arm Machine	$34.00		
Patterns:			
The Wave Lotus	$ 8.00		
Scrappy Wave Pattern	$ 8.00		
Tri Angle Waves Pattern	$ 8.00		
Waves in the Rail Pattern	$ 8.00		
Circles of Colors Pattern	$ 8.00		
Waves of Placemats/ Napkins Pattern	$ 8.00		
Books:			
Let's Make Waves	$24.00		
Tools:			
Invisi Grip	$ 6.00		
Tweezers 6"	$ 3.50		
	Total Items Price		
	CA. residents add 8.25% CA Tax		
	Total		

Name _____

Address _____

City _____ State _____ ZIP _____

Phone _____

Email _____

Prices subject to change without notice.